Modern
and 20th Century
Piano
Pieces

Presenting 22 compositions as written
by master composers.
Edited by Sam Raphling.

Index

Contents

Clair de Lune
(Moonlight)

La lune était sereine et jouait sur les flots.
La fenêtre enfin libre est ouverte à la brise;
La sultane regarde, et la mer qui se brise,
Là- bas, d'un flot d'argent brode les noirs flots.
(Victor Hugo " Les Orientales ")

Edward MacDowell, Op. 37, No. 1
(1861 - 1908)

Dans le Hamac
(In The Hammock)

Sara, belle d'indolence,
  Se balance,
Dans un hamac, au-dessus
Du bassin d'une fontaine
  Toute pleine
D'eau puisée à l'Ilyssus.
(Victor Hugo "Les Orientales.")

Edward MacDowell, Op. 37, No. 2

Allegretto con indolenza

Arabesque
(No. 1)

Claude Debussy
(1862－1918)

Andantino con moto

Arabesque
（No. 2）

Claude Debussy

Clair de Lune

Claude Debussy

Album Leaf

Alexander Scriabine Op. 45, No.1
(1872 - 1915)

Andante piacevole (♩=108)

Prelude

(G♯ Minor)

Serge Rachmaninoff, Op. 32, No. 12

(1873 - 1943)

Moment Musical

Serge Rachmaninoff, Op. 16, No. 3

Humoreske

Allegro vivace

Serge Rachmaninoff, Op. 10, No. 5

Andante

La Vallée Des Cloches
(Valley of the Bells from "Miroirs")

Maurice Ravel
(1875–1937)

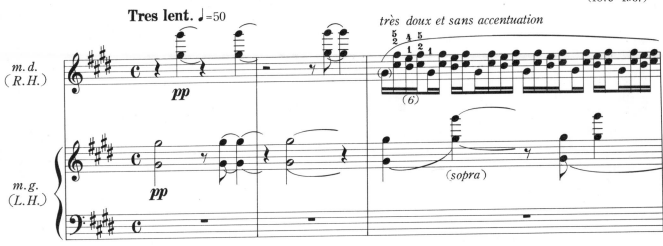

Pavane
(Pour Une Infante Défunte)

Maurice Ravel

Dolce, ma sempre sonoramente (♩=80)

Tempo I
come da lontano

Bear Dance

Béla Bartók
(1881 – 1945)

Etude

Andantino M.M. ♩. = 48

Igor Stravinsky, Op. 7, No. 3
(1882 –)

p *sempre con sordino*

sempr poco marc. ed espress.

(simile)

poco

poco

Mulatinha
(The Little Rubber Doll)

No.4 from
Prolé do Bébé No.1

Heitor Villa-Lobos
(1887—1959)

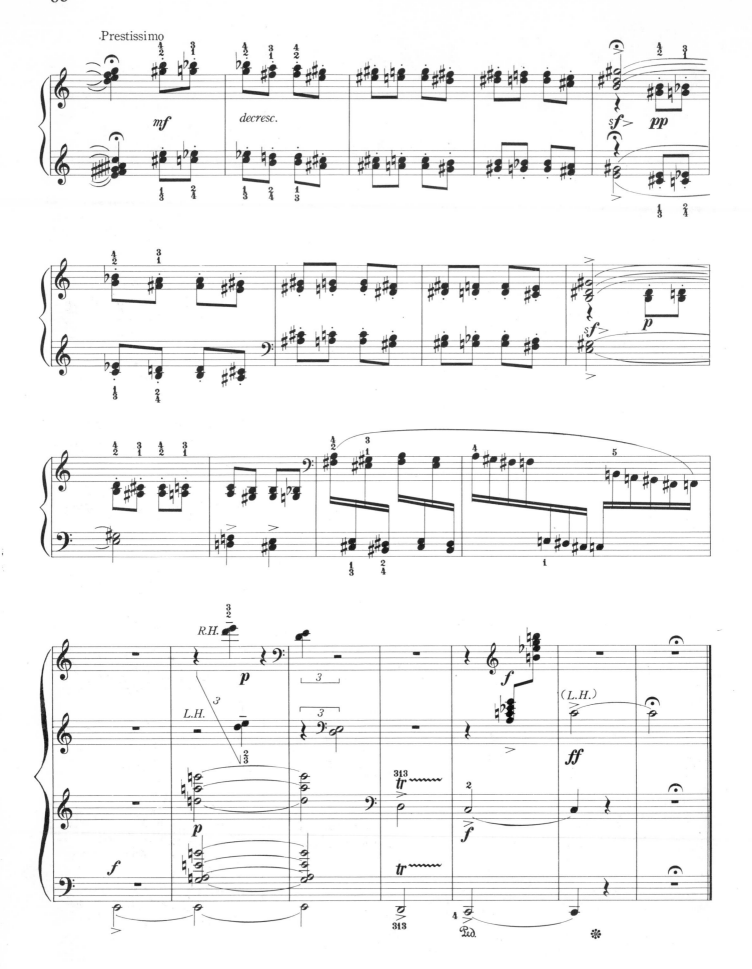

Prelude

Serge Prokofieff, Op. 12, No. 7
(1891–1953)

Vivo e delicato (♩=138)

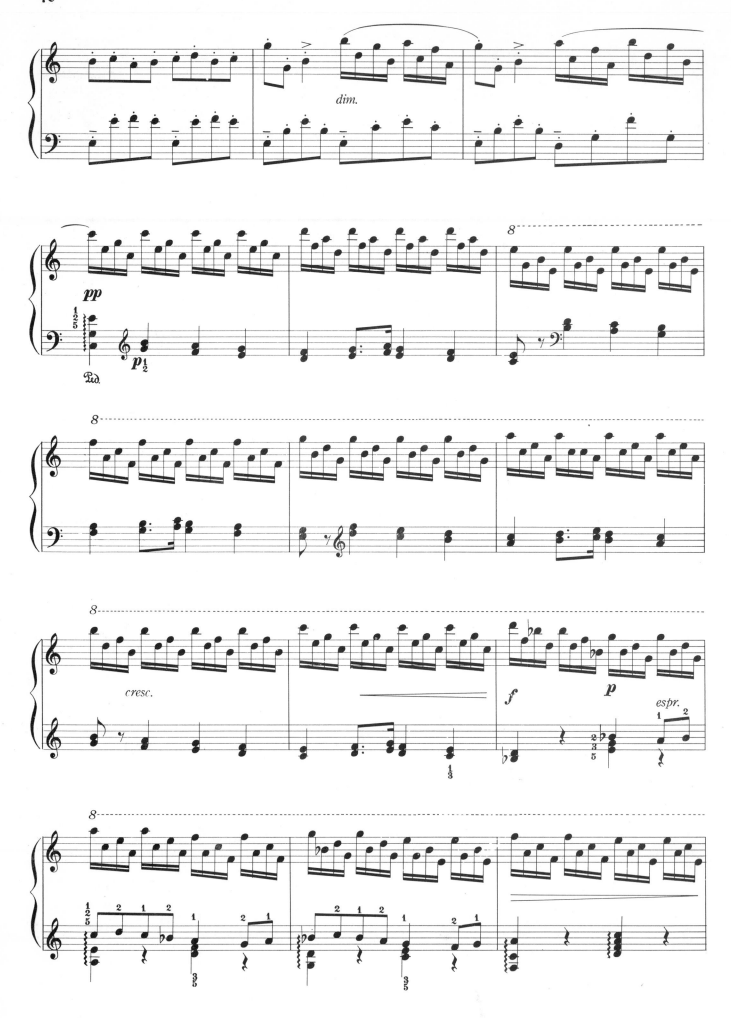

March
(from "Love For Three Oranges")

Serge Prokofieff, Op. 33

Toccata

Allegro marcatissimo ♩= 120

Aram Khatchaturian
(1903 –)

Vivace con brio

Andante espressivo

84

O Polichinelo

No. 1 from
Prolé do Bébé No. 1

Heitor Villa - Lobos

il canto distinto

Manquinha

(Little Lame Girl)

No. 74 from Album 1
of Guia Practico

Heitor Villa-Lobos

Variations No. 1
(Toccata)

Introduction

Allegretto brioso

Dmitri Kabalevsky Op. 40
(1904 -)

Var. 4

Var. 5

Var. 6

Var. 12 and Coda

3 Fantastic Dances

1

Dmitri Shostakovich, Op. 1
(1906 –)

2

3

Polka

(from "The Golden Age")

Allegretto (♩ = 84)

Dmitri Shostakovich